SIZZLING SAUSAGES

Written by
KATE RUTTLE

Illustrated by
SUE MASON

WAYLAND

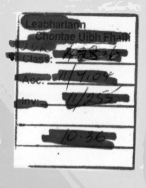

First published in 2011
by Wayland

Wayland
338 Euston Road
London NW1 3BH

Wayland Australia
Level 17/207 Kent Street
Sydney, NSW 2000

Series editor: Louise John
Designer: Paul Cherrill
Consultant: Kate Ruttle

A CIP catalogue record for this book is available
from the British Library.

ISBN 9780750262897

Printed in China

Wayland is a division of Hachette Children's Books,
an Hachette UK company. www.hachette.co.uk

FIZZ WIZZ PHONICS is a series of fun and exciting books, especially designed to be used by children who have not yet started to read.

The books support the development of language, exploring key speaking and listening skills, as well as encouraging confidence in pre-reading skills.

SIZZLING SAUSAGES is all about environmental sounds. The book tells the story of a day in the life of four-year-old Tom, beginning with Mum making sausages for breakfast in the kitchen. Then Tom, Mum and Baby have an eventful trip across town to meet Dad from the train. They return home for a lazy evening watching TV, before it is time for a bath and bed.

For suggestions on how to use **SIZZLING SAUSAGES** and further activities, look at page 24 of this book.

In the Kitchen

Early in the morning,
Tom is in the kitchen.

What can he see?
What can he hear?

In the Street

Tom goes out with
Mum and Baby.

What can he see?
What can he hear?

The Roadworks

Suddenly, the street is noisy.
Tom looks around him.

What can he see?
What can he hear?

In the Park

Now he's in the park
and Tom wants to play.

What can he see?
What can he hear?

At the Supermarket

After lunch, Tom helps
Mum with the shopping.

What can he see?
What can he hear?

At the Station

Ring, **ring**

Later in the afternoon,
Tom meets Dad after work.

What can he see?
What can he hear?

In the Sitting Room

Tom likes watching TV
after tea.

What can he see?
What can he hear?

In the Bathroom

Tom is getting ready
for bed.

What can he see?
What can he hear?

In the Bedroom

It's time for Tom
to go to sleep now.

What can he see?
What can he hear?

Night-time Garden

It's night-time. Tom looks out of his window.

What can he see?
What can he hear?

Further Activities

These activities can be used when reading the book one-to-one, or in the home.

P4 • What sounds can you hear in your kitchen?
   • Boil the kettle. Think about the sounds the kettle and the water make. Can you describe them?

P6 • Go for a short walk in the street. Talk about the sounds you hear. Which is the loudest sound? Which is the quietest?
   • Can you hear any weather? What kinds of sounds do you hear when it's windy, rainy or thundery?

P8 • Are there any roadworks nearby? If so, go and listen to them.
   • Use a tray to make a roadway out of cornflakes and oats. Listen to the sounds as toy vehicles are pushed over them.

P10 • Talk about the seasons. How do you know it's autumn in this book? What sounds are linked to autumn?
   • Go for a walk through the leaves. What kinds of sounds do the leaves make?

P12 • What happens when you knock over small stacks of different items: tins, packets etc. Which is noisier? Which is quieter?
   • Visit a supermarket to look at the people and listen to the sounds. Are people happy or sad? Are they relaxed or in a hurry?

P14 • Pack a suitcase with some towels. Drag it across different surfaces. Does the suitcase always make a noise?
   • Watch or read a story set in a train station. Look at the images for things that make sounds.

P16 • Watch a film together. Think about the noises you can hear as well as the sound of the characters talking.
   • Look at the roaring fire. Can you think of other words to describe the sound the fire might make?

P18 • Wash your hands and brush your teeth. What sort of noises are you making?
   • Listen to the sound as you turn a tap on from dripping, to running softly, to splashing loudly.

P20 • Sort toys into two groups: noisy toys and quiet toys. Talk about the kinds of noises the toys make. Can you describe the noises?

P22 • Draw pictures of nocturnal creatures. Find out what kinds of noises your creatures make.
   • Look out of the window and find things that might make a noise if the wind blew. What sounds would they make?

These activities can be used when using the book with more than one child, or in an educational setting.

P4 • Use kitchen play equipment. Listen to the sound of the toy toaster when a piece of 'toast' pops up. POP!
   • Talk about what might be in the frying pan. Can you make a sizzling noise?

P6 • Go outside and listen to the sounds of traffic passing. Do it again on a day with different weather. How does the weather make the traffic noise change?

P8 • Have you ever seen any roadworks? What sounds do they make?
   • Find pictures of the different machines used in roadworks.
   • Why do the men in the picture have protective ear coverings?

P10 • Model a play park from junk. Think of the sounds the equipment makes as it works.
   • What sounds do you make when you play on the equipment? Are they happy or sad sounds? Loud sounds or soft sounds?

P12 • Have you ever been into a supermarket? Is it a quiet or noisy place? Make a supermarket in your role play area, stacking shelves, tidying up and working on the till etc.

P14 • Look at the picture. Why are people at the station? Try to think of different reasons.
   • Use a train set to make a busy station scene. What makes a loud noise in the station? Which sounds are quieter?

P16 • Gather a selection of foods, for example crisps, bananas, grapes, carrots, bread, cucumber and jelly. Taste the different foods. Can you describe the sound the food makes when you eat it?

P18 • Play in the water tray, bathing dolls. What sounds do you make?
   • Talk about brushing teeth. Look at a normal and an electric toothbrush. Listen to the noise each one makes.

P20 • Make simple mobiles using milk bottle tops, tissue paper, jingle bells, teaspoons or carrots. Hang the mobiles up and listen to them as they move.

P22 • Talk about why Tom might be awake at night. Use the internet to find out what noises the animals in this picture might make. Can you mimic the noises?